WILL IT EVER CLOSE?

A book about the misadventures
of selling Real Estate!

by
Mari Mahoney
Brenda Haydock
&
Jacki McPherson

"WILL IT EVER CLOSE?"

Published by BWB Enterprises
Pleasanton, California
Third Printing

Cover by Michelle Domingo-Alexander
Color design by Jeff Reber
Desktop Publishing by PageWorks

Printed by Turner Printing
Oakland, California

DEDICATION

This book is dedicated to all real estate agents. We truly appreciate how hard you work to help people attain their dream of home ownership. We are proud to be associated with you. Thank You.

FOREWORD

What if it doesn't appraise? What if the buyers don't qualify? What if the sellers back out? What if...? What if...? These are some of the questions that every real estate agent has asked himself or herself at one time or another.

The three of us have been in the real estate industry for many years and have also experienced the ups, downs, highs, and lows of real estate.

This book is intended to be a humorous look at what real estate agents may, have, or could experience in their everyday activity. We all appreciate the effort it takes to make a transaction run smoothly. (Run smoothly? Is that possible?) The challenges may be different, but it all comes down to the final question: **Will it ever close?!**

WILL IT EVER CLOSE WHEN...

Your client buys a house that needs a little "TLC"—
*but the appraiser remarks
"Tile, Lumber, and Concrete."*

WILL IT EVER CLOSE WHEN...

Your client thinks the FNMA Community
Home Buyer Program means
"the neighbors pitch in."

WILL IT EVER CLOSE WHEN...

Your client says he's an entrepreneur—
mostly "preneur."

WILL IT EVER CLOSE WHEN...

Your flood-zoned property
is re-listed as ocean-front.

WILL IT EVER CLOSE WHEN...

You are previewing your clients' home
—they are so proud of their remodeling efforts—
and all you can think is,
"How am I ever going to sell this?"

WILL IT EVER CLOSE WHEN...

The ad states "Location, Location, Location"—
but it's missing the word
"WRONG."

WILL IT EVER CLOSE WHEN...

You pay to run your ad at your local supermarket—
*but they put your picture
on milk cartons, instead.*

WILL IT EVER CLOSE WHEN...

You have to tell your clients
they have champagne taste—
on a condo budget.

WILL IT EVER CLOSE WHEN...

You ask your clients
how much they're putting down—
*and they have to go look
under the mattress.*

WILL IT EVER CLOSE WHEN...

An ad that states
"For the family on the go"
forgot to include the words
"MOBILE HOME."

WILL IT EVER CLOSE WHEN...

You've been previewing homes with clients
all weekend—*and find out
they just wanted decorating ideas.*

WILL IT EVER CLOSE WHEN...

You didn't realize that
"Great Freeway Access"
really meant
"the driveway."

WILL IT EVER CLOSE WHEN...

The new agent in your office
listed more properties in one day
than you've listed all month.

WILL IT EVER CLOSE WHEN...

"Motivated Seller"
really means
"Please buy—no one else will."

WILL IT EVER CLOSE WHEN...

The *no* points, *no* appraisal fee, *no* lender fee, *no* escrow fee, *no* title fee, *no* tax service fee, *no* flood certification fee, fixed-rate loan *is a* **"NO GO."**

WILL IT EVER CLOSE WHEN...

Your clients want to add
five cousins to the loan.

WILL IT EVER CLOSE WHEN...

Your 30-day closing
just went into probate.

WILL IT EVER CLOSE WHEN...

The buyers and sellers
are quibbling over $500, won't budge—
then look at you.

WILL IT EVER CLOSE WHEN...

Your clients schedule their final walk-through
with their family—
and you have to rent a bus.

WILL IT EVER CLOSE WHEN...

Your client thought "FHA" financing
really meant
"Free House Available."

WILL IT EVER CLOSE WHEN...

You've spent six months looking for an outfit to wear
to the awards presentation—
*only to find three other people
wearing the same outfit.*

WILL IT EVER CLOSE WHEN...

You finally found the motivational tapes
you purchased three years ago—
*and realize
you just bought them again.*

WILL IT EVER CLOSE WHEN...

The day you decide to walk your area—
it rains.

WILL IT EVER CLOSE WHEN...

You walk into the title company—
and everyone picks up the phone.

WILL IT EVER CLOSE WHEN...

Your Relo
just bought
a FSBO.

WILL IT EVER CLOSE WHEN...

The new Realtor® in the office thinks
"The Thomas Guide®"
is someone who gives directions.

WILL IT EVER CLOSE WHEN...

"<u>Lots</u> for little"
really means
"<u>*little*</u> *for Lots.*"

FOR
SALE

WILL IT EVER CLOSE WHEN...

You refer a client to another agent—
*and it turns out to be
a million dollar deal.*

WILL IT EVER CLOSE WHEN...

The clients you've been working with for a year
*just decided to sign
a lease option.*

WILL IT EVER CLOSE WHEN...

Your all-cash buyer
was just seen on
"America's Most Wanted©."

WILL IT EVER CLOSE WHEN...

The appraiser
*appraises
the wrong house.*

WILL IT EVER CLOSE WHEN...

"Must Sell"
really means
"Desperate."

WILL IT EVER CLOSE WHEN...

The new Realtor® in the office
asks you for directions—
to his listing.

WILL IT EVER CLOSE WHEN...

Your 3% down, 2% gift,
10% carry back
exceeds 100% financing.

WILL IT EVER CLOSE WHEN...

The only calls you get
regarding your new listing
are nosy neighbors.

WILL IT EVER CLOSE WHEN...

You found your clients a house,
you're ready to make an offer—
*and the listing agent says,
"I'll have my people call your people."*

WILL IT EVER CLOSE WHEN...

Your best friend just bought a house—
from another Realtor®,
because she didn't want to bother you.

WILL IT EVER CLOSE WHEN...

The house you just previewed
with an "add-on"
should have been
a "tear-down."

WILL IT EVER CLOSE WHEN...

Your goal list
becomes target practice.

WILL IT EVER CLOSE WHEN...

Your client, who left California
because of all the earthquakes,
*just had his home
leveled by a tornado.*

WILL IT EVER CLOSE WHEN...

The seller says his house is 2,000 sq. ft.,
the assessor says 1,400 sq. ft.,
the appraiser says 1,000 sq. ft., and you say,
"I'm glad I have error and omissions insurance."

WILL IT EVER CLOSE WHEN...

"Executive living"
really means
"Condo for one."

WILL IT EVER CLOSE WHEN...

The hillside property your clients loved
just rolled down the hill.

WILL IT EVER CLOSE WHEN...

A referral from your best client
speaks a different language.

WILL IT EVER CLOSE WHEN...

You just found out
*your real estate license
has expired.*

WILL IT EVER CLOSE WHEN...

You've searched for six months;
your clients find the "perfect" home—
and it just sold!

WILL IT EVER CLOSE WHEN...

The underwriter
*laughed at the appraiser's
estimate of value.*

WILL IT EVER CLOSE WHEN...

You're in the business for so long
that you think you've seen it all—
but you're wrong.

WILL IT EVER CLOSE WHEN...

You have the <u>most</u> listings—
and the <u>least</u> cash.

WILL IT EVER CLOSE WHEN...

Your client can only sign
closing papers at 5:30 p.m.—
*but the office closes at 5:00 p.m.
and you are <u>not</u> a notary.*

WILL IT EVER CLOSE WHEN...

You are both the listing and
the selling agent—
and your clients are at a standstill.

WILL IT EVER CLOSE WHEN...

You get a counter offer
on your client's home—
for the 15th time.

WILL IT EVER CLOSE WHEN...

Your buyer gets buyer's remorse
six months after the closing—
*and wants to know
if he can back out of the deal.*

WILL IT EVER CLOSE WHEN...

Your client "kicks the bucket"—
before the closing.

WILL IT EVER CLOSE WHEN...

Your lender calls and says,
*"Do you want the good news
or the bad news?"*

WILL IT EVER CLOSE WHEN...

Property values just decreased—
for the fifth time this month.

WILL IT EVER CLOSE WHEN...

You get five offers on your listing—
*and your client
decides not to sell.*

WILL IT EVER CLOSE WHEN...

You already spent your commission—
*on the deal
that just fell through.*

WILL IT EVER CLOSE WHEN...

Your loan is approved,
you're ready to close—
*and the bank calls to say,
"There's one more condition."*

WILL IT EVER CLOSE WHEN...

The title rep calls you—
to pick up something for_him_.

WILL IT EVER CLOSE WHEN...

Your assistant
can't find your file.

WILL IT EVER CLOSE WHEN...

The house you just sold
with the "extended family room"
does not have permits.

WILL IT EVER CLOSE WHEN...

You just locked your keys in the car—
*in front of the buyer, the seller,
the listing broker, and your manager.*

WILL IT EVER CLOSE WHEN...

You have two clients show up
to preview property—
at the same time.

WILL IT EVER CLOSE WHEN...

While on caravan,
you see your best friend's house—
listed with another broker.

WILL IT EVER CLOSE WHEN...

The deal closes—
and the renters won't move.

WILL IT EVER CLOSE WHEN...

Your "fixer upper"
should have been
"down under."

WILL IT EVER CLOSE WHEN...

Your client threatens
to take his listing somewhere else—
and your first thought is,
"Go ahead...make my day!"

WILL IT EVER CLOSE WHEN...

The ad you ran states,
"No down payment needed"—
*and your client thinks it means
"No job needed."*

WILL IT EVER CLOSE WHEN...

You think you have the perfect client—
*but the bank says
they have all but perfect credit.*

WILL IT EVER CLOSE WHEN...

You lost a deal to another agent in your office—
*only to find out
he cut his commission.*

WILL IT EVER CLOSE WHEN...

Every house you showed on Friday
sold on Monday.

WILL IT EVER CLOSE WHEN...

The house you're trying to show
has no key in the lock box.

WILL IT EVER CLOSE WHEN...

Your client calls to tell you that
he forgot he has a second cousin,
twice removed, now remarried,
who is a Realtor®.

WILL IT EVER CLOSE WHEN...

Your clients, who had
no problem finding a home,
have no money.

WILL IT EVER CLOSE WHEN...

Your transaction is ready to close—
and no payoff demand was ordered.

WILL IT EVER CLOSE WHEN...

You return a client's page, only to hear,
"Don't worry! I found another agent."

WILL IT EVER CLOSE WHEN...

The property listed with a "Sparkling Pool"
neglects to include the words
"Some Assembly Required."

WILL IT EVER CLOSE WHEN...

The award you thought you were getting
just went to the new guy in the office.

WILL IT EVER CLOSE WHEN...

Your client neglects to tell you
*he is working with
two other Realtors® besides you.*

WILL IT EVER CLOSE WHEN...

The flyers you just picked up
from the printer
look like your kids drew them.

WILL IT EVER CLOSE WHEN...

Some days you feel more like
*the gardener, housekeeper,
mailman, plumber, and carpenter.*

WILL IT EVER CLOSE WHEN...

Almost all the farm cards you mailed
came back—
marked "Return to Sender."

WILL IT EVER CLOSE WHEN...

Your client decides not to lock in his rate.
It just went up—
and now he doesn't qualify.

WILL IT EVER CLOSE WHEN...

Your commission check
is inadvertently delivered to the listing agent—
and he cashes it.

WILL IT EVER CLOSE WHEN...

The house with the
maintenance-free landscape
doesn't have a yard.

WILL IT EVER CLOSE WHEN...

Your client thinks you are
part "gopher."

WILL IT EVER CLOSE WHEN...

Your closing papers arrive—
the day they expire.

WILL IT EVER CLOSE WHEN...

The bank promises a one-day
loan approval—
subject to 50 conditions.

WILL IT EVER CLOSE WHEN...

You drive 49 miles
for a listing presentation—
and you see another Realtor® leaving.

WILL IT EVER CLOSE WHEN...

You give away your floor time to have lunch—
*only to find out your replacement
booked five listings.*

WILL IT EVER CLOSE WHEN...

You meet a new client—
and you're out of business cards.

WILL IT EVER CLOSE WHEN...

You mark a file "RUSH"—
*only to find it
at the bottom of your assistant's stack.*

WILL IT EVER CLOSE WHEN...

Your client lost his job—
just before closing.

WILL IT EVER CLOSE WHEN...

You show up for your
10:30 a.m. listing appointment—
only to find out it was at 9:30 a.m.

WILL IT EVER CLOSE WHEN...

Your client thought your "VA" property
really meant
"Very Available."

WILL IT EVER CLOSE WHEN...

Your Sunday newspaper ads come out—
and all the properties advertised
are already sold.

WILL IT EVER CLOSE WHEN...

Your client's dream home
just became a nightmare.

WILL IT EVER CLOSE WHEN...

You just presented an offer for your clients,
but found out they made an offer
on another house—
without you.

WILL IT EVER CLOSE WHEN...

The ad you placed in the newspaper
has someone else's phone number.

WILL IT EVER CLOSE WHEN...

Your clients arrived at closing on time—
but their loan docs didn't.

WILL IT EVER CLOSE WHEN...

"Split Level"
really means
"Divorce in process."

WILL IT EVER CLOSE WHEN...

Your client decided to move—
into an apartment.

WILL IT EVER CLOSE WHEN...

The house down the street
*just listed $20,000 less than
your "priced to sell" listing.*

WILL IT EVER CLOSE WHEN...

The ad that states,
"Personal property included"
really means
"*Husband stays, too.*"

WILL IT EVER CLOSE WHEN...

The movers show up—
but the transaction hasn't closed.

WILL IT EVER CLOSE WHEN...

You spend all day at your open house—
and no one shows.

WILL IT EVER CLOSE WHEN...

The underwriter made
a quick loan decision—
NO!

WILL IT EVER CLOSE WHEN...

You drive by an expired listing
described as "One-of-a-Kind"—
and your first reaction is
"No wonder!"

WILL IT EVER CLOSE WHEN...

You take a new client to lunch,
forget your credit cards—
and you have no cash.

WILL IT EVER CLOSE WHEN...

The floor call
gave you a fake number.

WILL IT EVER CLOSE WHEN...

The house you found "As Is"
should have been
"*Never Was.*"

WILL IT EVER CLOSE WHEN...

The appraised value comes in low...

W
  A
    Y   L
        O
         W

WILL IT EVER CLOSE WHEN...

Some days you say to yourself,
"I shouldn't have left my day job."

WILL IT EVER CLOSE WHEN...

You have an "Open House" with no activity—
*only to find
someone had stolen all your signs.*

WILL IT EVER CLOSE WHEN...

The new Realtor® in the office passes the test the first time— *and it took you three times.*

WILL IT EVER CLOSE WHEN...

You preview a house that states,
"Remodeled Kitchen"—
and all that's new is the dishwasher.

WILL IT EVER CLOSE WHEN...

Your clients think you are a
personal taxi service.

WILL IT EVER CLOSE WHEN...

Your client calls to tell you the good news—
he just got his real estate license.

WILL IT EVER CLOSE WHEN...

Every floor call you get
just wants to lease.

WILL IT EVER CLOSE WHEN...

The property advertised with a "great view"
*was actually referring to the
naked neighbors.*

WILL IT EVER CLOSE WHEN...

You show a client $300,000 homes—
*but find
he can only qualify for $80,000.*

WILL IT EVER CLOSE WHEN...

Your client asks you
to reduce your commission—
and you say,
"Uhh...yes."

WILL IT EVER CLOSE WHEN...

Your sellers want <u>you</u>
to help fix up <u>their</u> home.

WILL IT EVER CLOSE WHEN...

The buyers and the sellers
won't sign the closing papers.

WILL IT EVER CLOSE WHEN...

You saw your favorite client at lunch—
with the #1 Realtor® in town.

WILL IT EVER CLOSE WHEN...

The C.M.A. you completed last night
is on the wrong property.

WILL IT EVER CLOSE WHEN...

You finally find the perfect home
your client can afford,
but the commute is three hours—
one way.

WILL IT EVER CLOSE WHEN...

You are ready for a great
three-day weekend—
and your lender calls at 4:47 p.m. to say,
"We've got a problem."

WILL IT EVER CLOSE WHEN...

You lose "Top Agent of the Year"—
by one sale.

WILL IT EVER CLOSE WHEN...

"Everything Included"
really meant
"everything except the kitchen sink."

WILL IT EVER CLOSE WHEN...

You are ready to close,
but find new judgements—
all 26 of them.

WILL IT EVER CLOSE WHEN...

You find that at your final walk-through,
the sellers walked off with everything.

WILL IT EVER CLOSE WHEN...

You are top listing agent for the month—
but none of your listings have sold.

WILL IT EVER CLOSE WHEN...

The bank's rates dropped—
and so did your client.

WILL IT EVER CLOSE WHEN...

Your clients expect you
to hold their home open—
every weekend.

WILL IT EVER CLOSE WHEN...

Your clients decided to refinance—
instead of sell.

WILL IT EVER CLOSE WHEN...

You get elected—
*to run
all the fund raisers.*

WILL IT EVER CLOSE WHEN...

You moved to a new office—
but your files didn't.

WILL IT EVER CLOSE WHEN...

Your clients get transferred—
midway through the sale.

WILL IT EVER CLOSE WHEN...

You waited all day to run your
client's property on the computer
and it went down—
again.

WILL IT EVER CLOSE WHEN...

Your contract says, "Owners will carry"—
but what they really mean is,
"their own furniture."

WILL IT EVER CLOSE WHEN...

Your clients decide to file bankruptcy—
halfway through the transaction.

WILL IT EVER CLOSE WHEN...

You are ready to close your sale—
and the concurrent deal falls through.

WILL IT EVER CLOSE WHEN...

The company you just left
merged with your new company.

WILL IT EVER CLOSE WHEN...

Even with co-signers,
your client won't qualify.

WILL IT EVER CLOSE WHEN...

You get to the bank on Friday
to cash your "BIG" commission check—
and find out it's NSF.

WILL IT EVER CLOSE WHEN...

You have six people trying
to buy a home—
but you need two more to qualify.

WILL IT EVER CLOSE WHEN...

The ad states "Newly painted"—
it really meant
"New graffiti."

WILL IT EVER CLOSE WHEN...

It's your floor time—
and the walk-ins just walked out!

WILL IT EVER CLOSE WHEN...

Your clients make an offer
on their "Dream Home"—
and the bank told them to "Dream On."

WILL IT EVER CLOSE WHEN...

Your assistant calls in sick—
for a week.

WILL IT EVER CLOSE WHEN...

You pay someone to walk your area
and pass out flyers—
and he leaves them all on one doorstep.

WILL IT EVER CLOSE WHEN...

You listed a foreclosure—
and the bank sold it without you.

WILL IT EVER CLOSE WHEN...

The business cards you just ordered
have the wrong area code.

WILL IT EVER CLOSE WHEN...

Someone broke something—
at your "Broker's Open."

WILL IT EVER CLOSE WHEN...

You see an ad in the paper that states,
"New Tract"—
but it forgot to include the word
"Railroad."

WILL IT EVER CLOSE WHEN...

You finally find the perfect home for your clients—
*but the address is 13 Thirteenth Street
and your clients are very superstitious.*

WILL IT EVER CLOSE WHEN...

Your buyer's loan commitment
is about to expire—
*and all the computers
are down for the entire day.*

WILL IT EVER CLOSE WHEN...

Your full-price offer
is not accepted.

WILL IT EVER CLOSE WHEN...

You run out of gas with your
clients in the car—
and it is 100° outside.

WILL IT EVER CLOSE WHEN...

Your "Full of cash" clients
turn out to be
"Full of hot air."

WILL IT EVER CLOSE WHEN...

You are always a day late—
and a listing short.

WILL IT EVER CLOSE WHEN...

Your client sends flowers to your office—
but they're not for you.

WILL IT EVER CLOSE WHEN...

Your seller
won't fix a thing.

WILL IT EVER CLOSE WHEN...

Your floor time
is just a waste of time.

WILL IT EVER CLOSE WHEN...

Your client has 30% down—
but he can't remember where he got it.

WILL IT EVER CLOSE WHEN...

Title reps
won't even return your calls.

WILL IT EVER CLOSE WHEN...

Your client didn't take the first offer—
and it was the last.

WILL IT EVER CLOSE WHEN...

The motivational seminar you took
is working for everyone else.

WILL IT EVER CLOSE WHEN...

Your sellers
despise Real Estate Agents.

WILL IT EVER CLOSE WHEN...

Just before your transaction closed,
your clients bought a new car—
and the bank found out.

WILL IT EVER CLOSE WHEN...

The judge forced a divorce sale—
and your clients got back together.

WILL IT EVER CLOSE WHEN...

The Federal Reserve
thinks the recession is over.

WILL IT EVER CLOSE WHEN...

The market starts moving—
but your clients won't.

WILL IT EVER CLOSE WHEN...

Your Number-One Builder
has a new subdivision and a new girlfriend—
who happens to have a real estate license.

WILL IT EVER CLOSE WHEN...

The property described as "A Doll House"
is really referring to its size.

WILL IT EVER CLOSE WHEN...

The only listing you have
won't sell.

WILL IT EVER CLOSE WHEN...

Your client thinks "MLS"
stands for
"Makes Little Sense."

WILL IT EVER CLOSE WHEN...

The title company
recorded the wrong deed.

WILL IT EVER CLOSE WHEN...

Your client shows up
for your appointment to look at property—
wearing the same shirt and tie as you.

WILL IT EVER CLOSE WHEN...

Your client doesn't just want zero down—
but also zero points and zero payments.

WILL IT EVER CLOSE WHEN...

The ad states "Decorator's Dream"—
your first thought is,
"In your dreams."

WILL IT EVER CLOSE WHEN...

Your five sales from last month
all fell through this month.

WILL IT EVER CLOSE WHEN...

Your listing is located "in the woods"—
*but you need a four-wheel drive
to get there.*

ABOUT THE AUTHORS

Mari Mahoney has for the last seventeen years enjoyed a successful career in mortgage banking and is currently a nationally-recognized professional speaker in that industry.

Brenda Haydock started her career in real estate with the Department of Veterans Affairs and moved on to become a successful independent real estate appraiser in California for the last seventeen years.

Jacki McPherson has been a top producing mortgage broker in Southern California for the last ten years.

ORDER FORM

If you would like to order additional copies of "Will It Ever Close?" fill out the order form below and send or fax to:

BWB Enterprises
4847 Hopyard Road. #3161
Pleasanton, California 94588
Fax (510) 484-4145

NAME: _____

ADDRESS: _____

CITY: _____ STATE: _____ ZIP: _____

PHONE: ( ) _____

Number of copies wanted: _____